Dedicated to Quarantine 2020

Health is Wealth

Vegan Fish from Banana Blossoms

- banana blossoms
- for the flour mixture: flour, salt, nori, dill
- for the batter: flour, salt, turmeric, pickle juice, caper brine (or more pickle juice), water, lemon juice
- frying oil Step 1: Rinse and drain the banana blossoms. Prepare the flour mixture and batter

Step 2: Coat the banana blossoms in the flour mixture.

Step 3: Dip the banana blossoms in the batter.

Step 4: Fry until golden. Place it on a kitchen paper to remove excess oil.

Side Note: Marinade Banana Blossoms in nori, dill,dash of fish oil for 30 mins or longer for a stronger fish taste

That boy is up to something

Same texture as real fish 🔥🔥🔥 WOW

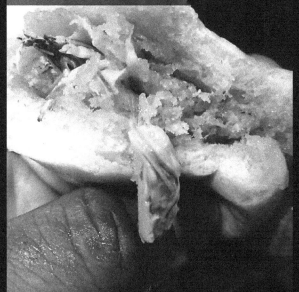

Grapefruit Rind Chicken Strips

Ingredients

- 2-3 red or pink grapefruits
- 2 cups double strength vegetarian chicken-style broth
- 2 garlic cloves, minced
- 2 eggs worth of egg replacer (I used The Vegg Baking mix)
- ½ tsp sea salt+ extra for seasoning
- ½ tsp black grounded pepper + extra for seasoning
- 1 tsp dried parsley
- 1 cup bread crumbs

Instructions

1. Peel the grapefruit and cut it in half. Separate the pulp from the piths (the piths will be used to cook the "chicken") with a spoon and your fingers. Try to keep the piths in one piece when cutting them off the fruit. Also, try the best you can not to get juice onto the grapefruit.
2. Cut the piths in half, they will be roughly the size of a normal schnitzel.
3. Bring a large pot of water to a boil and blanch the piths for about 15 minutes.
4. Remove the piths from the water and squeeze almost all the water out of the pith (without squishing it) and then repeat 4-5 times with COLD water, until the pith is no longer extremely bitter. You will have to be very careful not to over cook it, or else the texture will become literal mush.
5. Transfer the piths to a bowl, and cover with the double strength broth. Try to allow the piths to marinate for 1-hour or overnight for best results.
6. Remove the piths from the broth and allow to drain. The piths are very absorbent, so make sure you squeeze out all the marinade. You want the pieces to be almost DRY, otherwise the frying experience with be horrible, and you'll have soggy pieces.
7. Rub both sides of the piths with minced garlic and season with salt and pepper.
8. Mix the egg replacer, ½ tsp salt, ½ tsp black pepper and dried parsley together.
9. Dip the piths in the mixture, and then cover both sides in bread crumbs and place on a cooling rack to rest.
10. Heat up your oil to 365F, and line a baking sheet, as the peels rest.
11. Carefully lower the peels into the hot oil, cooking in batches.
12. Fry until golden brown, and heated through, about 1-2 minutes on each side.
13. Serve immediately with a dipping sauce of your choice.

INGREDIENTS

Buffalo cauliflower:

- 1 Head of cauliflower
- 2 cups white whole wheat flour
- ½ cup vegan Buffalo Hot Sauce
- 1 cup of a plant based milk
- ½ cup filtered water
- 1 tsp ground cayenne pepper
- 1 tsp fresh ground black pepper
- 1 tsp ground white pepper
- 1 tsp garlic powder
- 1 tsp smoked paprika
- 1 tsp turmeric

Creamy ranch dressing:

- 1 cup silken tofu
- 1 tsp lemon juice
- 1 clove garlic
- ½ tsp black pepper
- 1/4 tsp onion powder
- 1 1/4 tsp apple cider vinegar
- 1/2-1 tsp maple syrup
- 1 tbsp fresh minced dill (or 2 tsp dried)
- 1 tbsp fresh minced parsley
- 1 tsp chives

INSTRUCTIONS

For the buffalo cauliflower:

1. Preheat oven to 400 degrees fahrenheit / 200 degree celsius
2. Line a 15" x 9" sheet pan with a silicon mat or parchment paper
3. Trim the cauliflower and cut into 1.5" – 2" pieces, set aside
4. In a large mixing bowl combine all dry ingredients and mix thoroughly
5. In a large mixing bowl add your plant based milk and filtered water
6. Using a handful at a time, dip the cauliflower into the plant based milk making sure each piece is wet. Shake off excess liquid and immediately add to the seasoned whole wheat white flour and toss until each piece is coated
7. Transfer coated cauliflower pieces to a small strainer and lightly shake over the seasoned flour mixture so the excess falls back into the seasoned flour mix. Once done, evenly arrange the coated cauliflower to the lined sheet pan and place into the preheated over for 20 minutes
8. After 20 minutes remove the cauliflower from the oven and place in a large mixing bowl
9. Add the hot sauce and mix lightly making sure each piece is coated
10. Return the sauced cauliflower to the sheet pan and place back into the oven for another 20 minutes
11. After 20 minutes remove and enjoy!

For the creamy ranch dressing:

- Add all ingredient except for the herbs to a high speed blender
- Blend on high for 1 minute or until very creamy and smooth.
- Pour into a bowl and fold in the herbs. Enjoy!

Black Bean Burger

Ingredients

- 1 (15 ounce) can black beans, drained and rinsed
- 1/3 cup chopped sweet onion
- 1 tablespoon minced garlic
- 3 baby carrots, grated (optional)
- 1/4 cup minced green bell pepper (optional)
- 1 tablespoon cornstarch
- 1 tablespoon warm water
- 3 tablespoons chile-garlic sauce (such as Sriracha®), or to taste
- 1 teaspoon chili powder
- 1 teaspoon ground cumin
- 1 teaspoon seafood seasoning (such as Old Bay®)
- 1/4 teaspoon salt
- 1/4 teaspoon ground black pepper
- 2 slices whole-wheat bread, torn into small crumbs
- 3/4 cup unbleached flour, or as needed
- Add all ingredients to list

Direction

Preheat oven to 350 degrees F (175 degrees C). Grease a baking sheet. Mash black beans in a bowl; add onion, garlic, carrots, and green bell pepper. Mix. Whisk cornstarch, water, chile-garlic sauce, chili powder, cumin, seafood seasoning, salt, and black pepper together in a separate small bowl. Stir cornstarch mixture into black bean mixture. Mix whole-wheat bread into bean mixture. Stir flour, 1/4 cup at a time, into bean mixture until a sticky batter forms. Spoon 'burger-sized' mounds of batter onto the prepared baking sheet, about a 3/4-inch thickness per mound. Shape into burgers. Bake in the preheated oven until cooked in the center and crisp in the outside, about 10 minutes on each side.

Cheese sauce

INGREDIENTS

- Two large Yukon gold potatoes - medium cubed (1 inch)
- One medium carrot medium cubed (1 inch)
- 2 cups of filtered water
- 1/4 cup of soaked raw cashews
- 2 tbsp nutritional yeast
- 1/2 jalapeño - seeds included
- 1 clove of fresh minced garlic (oil free if using jarred)
- ½ tsp turmeric
- 1 tsp ground black pepper
- ½ tsp onion powder
- 1 tsp smoked paprika

INSTRUCTIONS

Add the carrots and potatoes to the 2 cups of water and bring to a boil for 4 minutes. Turn off the heat and let the potatoes and carrots sit in the water for 10 minutes. Strain but reserve the water. Add all ingredients (minus the reserved water) to a Vitamix or other high speed mixer. Start in a low speed gradually working your way up to high as you add in small amounts the reserved water. Blend until desired consistency - approximately 1 minute. Note - you may not need to use all of the reserved water. Once blended set aside 1/2 cup for later use.

Smoked tempeh

ING

- 8 oz of tempeh
- 2 tbsp maple syrup
- 1 tsp liquid smoke
- 2 tsp aminos

INSTRUCTIONS

Start by breaking up the tempeh into small chunks. Then place the tempeh into a food processor and pulse a few times or until ground. Add all ingredients to a large mixing bowl and incorporate. Set in refrigerator to marinade for up to 1 hour.

1. Preheat oven to 375 degrees.
2. Cook off one box (9 oz) of red lentil macaroni (optional choices based on preferences) for 7 minutes then strain with cold water and let drip dry for 1 minute.
3. Add all ingredients together (except the 1/2 cup of saved cheese sauce) in a large mixing bowl. Fold until incorporated evenly
4. Add to oven safe casserole pan and cover with lid or aluminum foil
5. Cook for 5 minutes and remove from oven
6. Sprinkle the top with bread crumbs if so desired (you can make your own whole wheat bread crumbs!)
7. Place back in oven and set the broiler for 3 minutes checking frequently to make sure the top isn't burning
8. Just looking for a crisp crunchy top
9. Remove from oven and allow to cool for 5 minutes then scoop out your portion! At this point I like to drizzle the saved cheese sauce and just a little of my Hamsa Hot Sauce over the top!

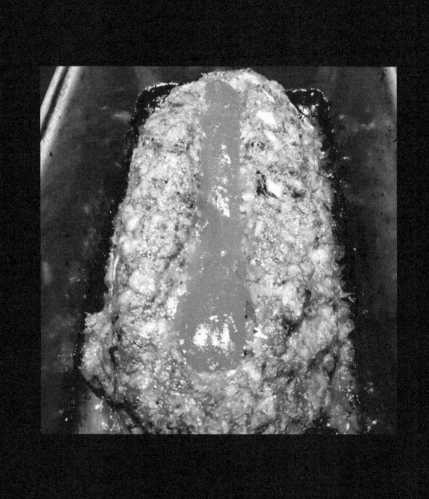

Meatless Meatloaf

Ingredients

VEGETABLES FOR SAUTÉING

- 1-2 tablespoons olive oil OR water for oil free
- 1 small onion, diced small
- 2 small carrots, diced small
- 2 celery stalks, diced small
- 3 garlic cloves, minced

FOR THE REST

- (2) 15 oz cans chickpeas, drained and rinsed, *(3 cups)*
- 1- 1 1/2 cups breadcrumbs*
- 2 tablespoons ground flaxseed
- 3 tablespoons nutritional yeast
- 2 tablespoons soy sauce
- 2 tablespoons vegan Worcestershire sauce
- 1/4 cup ketchup
- 1/2 teaspoon liquid smoke, optional, but good

FOR THE TOPPING

- 1/3 cup ketchup
- 1 teaspoon vegan Worcestershire sauce

Instructions

- Preheat the oven to 375 degrees and lightly spray a 9 inch loaf pan with oil, or line the bottom with parchment paper to prevent sticking.
- Saute the onion, carrots, celery and garlic in the olive oil or water over medium heat for 5 minutes, until the onions are translucent. Remove from heat and set aside.
- Add the chickpeas to a large bowl, and mash with a potato masher (or fork). You do not want them to be completely pasty or mushy, but well broken up. *Alternatively, use a food processor, but be careful not to over blend them and make them totally mushy. Pulse a couple of times if using a food processor.*
- Add the cooked veggies and all the remaining ingredients to the chickpeas. I have found 1 cup of breadcrumbs to be enough, but if the mixture seems really moist, add an extra 1/2 cup. Stir with a large wooden spoon until very well combined.
- Press the loaf mixture in the prepared pan, pushing down evenly with your hand. Cover with foil and bake for 30 minutes.
- In a small bowl, stir together the ketchup and Worcestershire sauce for the topping.
- After 30 minutes, remove the foil, spread the ketchup topping evenly on top of the loaf and bake for another 15 minutes, uncovered. Remove from the oven.
- Allow to sit for at least 15 minutes before slicing if you can, it will hold up better. Sprinkle with fresh parsley if desired before serving.

INGREDIENTS

- 1/2 yellow onion, finely chopped
- 1 tablespoon oil
- 1 (15 ounce) can black beans, drained and rinsed
- 1 (8 ounce) block tempeh, broken by hand into small pieces
- 1 tablespoon hot sauce
- 2 tablespoons cornstarch, or potato starch
- 2 tablespoons flour
- 1 teaspoon salt
- 3 tablespoons fresh chopped parsley
- 1 teaspoon cumin
- 1/2 teaspoon smoked paprika
- Black pepper, To Taste
- Garlic powder, To Taste
- 4 burger buns
- Ketchup, for topping
- Mustard, for topping
- Avocado mayonnaise, for topping

INSTRUCTIONS

Heat the oil in a pan over medium heat. Sauté the onion until translucent, then remove from heat.

Mix everything together in a food processor, except for the starch and flour.

Place the mixture in a bowl, thoroughly combine the starch and flour, then shape into patties.

Cook them in the oven at 400°F for about 20-25 minutes (flipping halfway through) or in a non stick pan over medium heat for about 3 minutes per side. Enjoy!!!

Easy 5 Minute Vegan Tacos

Ingredients
- 4 whole wheat tortillas
- 1 grilled corn on the cob, husked or canned corn equivalent
- 1 cup or 170 grams cooked black beans
- 1 avocado, sliced
- 3/4 cup or 120 grams quartered cherry tomatoes
- 1/2 red onion, chopped
- 2 tablespoons fresh chopped parsley
- 1 teaspoon ground cumin
- 4 lime wedges
- salt and freshly ground black pepper to taste
- your favorite hot chili sauce, to taste

Instructions
- Assemble your tacos: Distribute corn, black beans, avocado slices, quartered cherry tomatoes, chopped onion and parsley among tortillas. Season with ground cumin, lime juice, salt and freshly ground black pepper. Drizzle with your favorite hot chili sauce. Enjoy!

Mexican Quinoa

Ingredients

- 2 1/4 cups water
- 1 1/2 cups quinoa
- 15 oz. can diced tomatoes with jalapeños or fire-roasted diced tomatoes, not drained
- 15 oz. can black beans, drained and rinsed
- 15 oz. can corn, drained
- 1 tablespoon fresh lime juice
- Spices to taste: I used 1/2 teaspoon chili powder, 1/4 teaspoon black pepper, 1/4 teaspoon salt, 1/4 teaspoon garlic powder, & 1/4 teaspoon cayenne pepper, plus 1 tablespoon chopped fresh cilantro
- Toppings: guacamole, salsa, sour cream or plain Greek yogurt, cheese, etc.

Instructions

- Add quinoa, water, and diced tomatoes to a medium skillet or saucepan. Bring liquid to a boil and reduce heat to simmer on medium-low, for 12-18 minutes or until quinoa is done (it "pops" open) and liquid is absorbed. Add an additional splash of water while cooking, if needed.
- Stir in black beans, corn, lime juice, and spices to taste.
- Spoon into bowls and serve warm with guacamole, salsa, sour cream or plain Greek yogurt, cheese, etc.
- Store leftovers in fridge for up to five days and serve warm or cold.

NUTRITION

Lemon One Pot Pasta

Ingredients

- 8 oz spaghetti (not gluten-free)*
- 2.25 cups *vegetable broth* plus more if needed
- 2 leeks (lower, lighter part only) chopped
- 1 cup chickpeas drained and rinsed
- juice of 1-1.5 lemons (start with one and then add more at the end)
- 2.5 tbsp *nutritional yeast*
- 1/2 tbsp *garlic powder*
- 1/2 tbsp *onion powder*
- 1 tsp *Dijon mustard*
- 1/2 cup frozen peas
- 1 large handful spinach

Instructions

1. Add all ingredients except peas and spinach to large saute pan or pot and bring to a boil. I use a saute pan so that the spaghetti fits across the bottom.

2. Turn down heat to medium and cook until pasta is almost done to your liking (about 10 mins), stirring occasionally. If you notice you need more broth, feel free to add more as you see fit.

3. Add in peas and spinach and cook for a few minutes until peas are heated through and pasta is at the perfect consistency for you (some people like pasta more all dente than others).

4. Top with my Vegan Parmesan and enjoy!

Vegan Gnocchi

- store-bought gnocchi
- spinach
- tomatoes
- garlic
- cashews (unsalted and not roasted)
- nutritional yeast
- miso
- mustard
- tapioca starch
- unsweetened almond milk
- salt and pepper

You need **only six ingredients for the vegan gnocchi sauce**:

1. cashews
2. nutritional yeast
3. white or yellow miso paste
4. Dijon mustard
5. tapioca starch
6. garlic

INSTRUCTIONS

Prepare the gnocchi according to the instructions on the package. Place the spinach in a colander and drain the gnocchi over it (this is an easy trick to wilt fresh spinach). Make the sauce: place all ingredients in a high speed blender and process until smooth. Pour the sauce into a large pot and heat until it thickens up. Add the gnocchi, the spinach, and the diced tomatoes. Cook for another minute.

NOTES

You will need a good blender to make the vegan gnocchi sauce. Otherwise it won't get as creamy.

- If you don't have a high speed blender, soaking the cashews over night helps a lot. Otherwise you don't have to worry about soaking them. I use a vitamix and I never soak my cashews for vegan cheese sauces.

CPSIA information can be obtained
at www.ICGtesting.com
Printed in the USA
LVHW070807200121
676904LV00048BA/1262